The Guiding Philosophy for the Future of Healthcare: It's Not What You Think...

(Actually It Is What You Think!)

The Guiding Philosophy for the Future of Healthcare: It's Not What You Think...

(Actually It Is What You Think!)

Nancy J. Gordon, Ph.D.

BOOKS

Winchester, UK
Washington, USA

First published by O-Books, 2012
O-Books is an imprint of John Hunt Publishing Ltd., Laurel House, Station Approach,
Alresford, Hants, SO24 9JH, UK
office1@o-books.net
www.o-books.com

For distributor details and how to order please visit the 'Ordering' section on our website.

Text copyright: Nancy J. Gordon 2011

ISBN: 978 1 84694 910 4

A CIP catalogue record for this book is available from the British Library.

Design: Lee Nash

Printed and bound by CPI Group (UK) Ltd, Croydon, CR0 4YY
Printed in the USA by Offset Paperback Mfrs, Inc

We operate a distinctive and ethical publishing philosophy in all
areas of our business, from our global network of authors to
production and worldwide distribution.

CONTENTS

Preface

How things actually work in this world is something I have questioned from childhood. Do we experience situations in life as the result of some sort of "randomness" or do we somehow play a role in creating our experiences? Does what we experience in life somehow affect other things and other people? These questions and more are what led me on a search for the "missing pieces" in our current understanding and explanation of how to become healthy and whole.

As a child growing up in the mountains of western North Carolina I always felt very connected to the "out doors." I was happiest when playing outside in the woods or creek. I would spend hours lying in the grass looking up at the sky feeling as though I was a part of everything I could see. Even at this young age I was keenly aware that there had to be more to the *world* than what I could see, touch, and prove. My sense of connection to animals and the Earth was not something that I could prove yet I felt it deep down in my soul.

As I got older I became aware of the fact that there had to be more to *life* than working, eating, and sleeping. There had to be a deeper meaning or purpose ...a plan of some sort that allowed me to leave the world a better place for having been here.

I continuously wondered what was missing from the formula of how to live a healthy, happy, fulfilling life? Eventually my search for answers led me to the fields of physics and psychoneuroimmunology. It was at this point when I realized the affect of our thoughts, feelings, attitudes, and beliefs on the body was one of the "missing pieces" in healthcare today.

It became perfectly clear to me that there was more to *health and well-being* than just diet, exercise, pills, and surgery. I knew of people who ate healthy and exercised regularly, yet died from some sort of heart condition or cancer at an early age. I had situations in my own life where the deciding factor over whether I got well, or not, was not the pills or the surgery, but my unwavering belief that I would heal.

This book is an attempt to put back these "missing pieces" into healthcare. It was written for both healthcare practitioners and their patients (all of us). In other words, it is for everyone who currently occupies a body and wants to be healthy and whole. In order to change healthcare for the better we *all* must first change our beliefs about what *creates health* before we will actually *change* how we *conduct* and *participate* in healthcare.

The time has come to create a *new philosophy* that focuses on a more holistic approach to healthcare— one that is built on the concept that the body-mind-spirit is one thing—fully connected. We must shift our focus from *treatment* to *prevention* in a way that puts each one of us back in the driver's seat of our own health and well-being. This shift will happen only when we clearly understand how to use our thoughts, emotions, and beliefs as *tools* to help create health and wellness. The time has come when we must broaden the scope of Western medicine to incorporate this concept into how we provide and participate in healthcare. Until we are willing to step outside the traditional medical box to look at this phenomenon, we are going to continue to struggle in our healthcare.

Acknowledgements

To my parents for their continued love, encouragement, and support. To my friends, Vicky and Jim Anthony (founders and CEO of the Cliffs Communities in Western North and South Carolina—www.cliffs-communities.com) for their love, support, and belief in me and for affording me the opportunity to help create the *best wellness experience* for the Cliffs Communities property owners and associates. I want to thank Cherie Stine for her help in coming up with the title to my book. Finally, to Holly Berry for her wisdom and willingness in preparing my manuscript.

Author's Note

There are three disclaimers that I want to share with you from the start. I am in the business of helping people become the best they can be; therefore, I can not be in the "beat up" business at the same time. The following three disclaimers apply throughout this book:

1. The word "blame" does not exist in my vocabulary. At no time am I ever blaming anyone for anything that is going on in their body or life. In order for people to become the best they can be they need more accurate information on how the world actually works. My role is to give people ALL the information so that they may use it to reach their full potential.

2. At no time am I ever implying that you should not use the best of Western medicine. Instead I am pointing out the limitation of our healthcare when practitioners do not understand energy and how it affects the body/mind/spirit.

3. At no time am I trying to replace Western medicine, instead of I am simply trying to broaden the scope from which most practitioners operate to include the concept of how thoughts, feeling, beliefs, intentions, and attitudes all have a profound affect on health and well-being.

Side note: When I use the term "body" throughout the paper I am referring to body/mind/spirit as one entity.

Side note: The word "affect" is used as a verb implying action.

Introduction

We are living in an exciting yet challenging time. Upon first glance, looking through the lens of "lack and limitation", we see a world characterized by much uncertainty— in the healthcare system, educational systems, politics, and the stock market, just to name a few. Through this lens we see an increase in the unemployment rates, inflation, divorce, violence, crime, hunger, poverty, and the overall level of fear.

Using this lens it would be easy to focus on all the things that are not right with the world, in fact many people are conditioned to think this way; however, all of this lack and limitation exists on only one level, the physical level. On this level "problems" are created with the mindset of lack and limitation, and life is viewed as a struggle. When this happens, stress is inevitable!

Stress has become a household name in the 21st Century. Stress is not a new thing as it has been around for centuries; it is only now that we are more aware of how much it affects us. Since the 1960's there has been a growing recognition that while stress is an inevitable part of our life, it is our *perception* of the situation, our *perception* of our ability to handle the situation, and finally our response to it, that determines the outcome. In other words, what we think about ourselves and our situations has a huge affect on not only what happens in our body but in our life.

Many doctors are now linking stress to numerous physical conditions in the body but the concept of how stress, in the form of fears, anxieties, worries, concerns, hopelessness, anger, and frustration, actually affects us physically is not fully understood by most people; therefore, we are at a standstill as to how to treat it. Many practitioners in Western medicine are not equipped to deal with *"the whole person"* instead they are taught to deal with numbers generated from tests that help to explain the symptoms of the disease.

* * *

Taking a second glance, and viewing the world through the lens of "unlimited possibilities," we see a completely different picture. Through this lens, we see a world where all things are possible. It is at this higher level of consciousness where visions and dreams exist as *energy* waiting to be molded into the physical world by our thoughts, beliefs, intentions, and perceptions.

In the 21st Century, Albert Einstein's theory of how the world works is the most widely accepted scientific explanation outside of Western medicine. This theory states that matter (physical) and energy (non-physical) is the same thing at the sub-atomic level. Einstein contends that everything is *connected* and *always in motion* (always vibrating); however, much of our present-day medical model is deeply rooted in Isaac

Newton's model in which the universe is viewed as a grand clock. This clock was made up of *solid, stationary* pieces and parts that are *separate* from one another. As you can see these theories are "polar opposites."

Newton's model was very important to the advancements made during the Industrial Revolution; however, scientists have discovered forces/energy such as electricity and magnetism that cannot be explained using the Newton's outdated model.

While Western medicine is firmly rooted in Newton's physics for the most part, we are beginning to see a few champions in the medical profession who are willing to step out of their traditional role to look at how thoughts and emotions affect the physical.

At the top of this list is Dr. Larry Dossey, a brilliant physician and one of the leading authorities in the world on holistic (body, mind, spirit) health. Dr. Dossey has written numerous books about the importance of practitioners understanding that a patient's perceptions, thoughts, feeling, and beliefs all have a significant impact on health and illness.

Dr. Dossey understands that positive emotions such as love, gratitude, and giving to others, have a positive affect on our health and well-being. He points out that by helping others we in fact are able to help our self to heal. We have all experienced the "physical effects" of these positive emotions in our own lives; however, we are reluctant to apply this when it comes to Western medicine.

In looking for research findings that show the

power of thoughts and expectations to help the body heal, one does not have to look much further than the studies around the phenomenon of the placebo. Medical researchers have been increasingly amazed by the fact that many people, when told of the side effects or reactions that will occur as a result of taking a medication, will experience those effects even when the medication is replaced with a pill containing sugar or saline. This clearly shows that expectations, thoughts, perceptions, and attitudes play a huge role in creating physical changes in the body; yet the application of this phenomenon has been removed from our current healthcare model.

The time has come to take a good look at our nation's understanding and response to the healthcare needs of its people. We must broaden the scope of Western medicine to create a more holistic model of care that focuses on enhancing health and not eliminating disease.

Holistic medicine, which is a modern day term for the mind, body, and spirit connection, emphasizes the role of the mind (thoughts, emotions, perceptions, and beliefs) in the health of the whole person. Advocates of holistic medicine do not want to replace traditional Western medicine but believe that by itself it is not enough to create genuine health and well-being.

One of the major challenges we face in the United States is that when most people think of "wellness" they only think of diet, exercise, and rest. Yet, from a holistic perspective, wellness must be defined in a way that includes all aspects of body-mind-spirit. The definition of wellness must be broad enough to include the benefits of living life with joy and gratitude, deep breathing, meditating, getting out in nature, being involved in loving relationships, choosing a positive outlook on oneself and the world, rest and relaxation, playing, spending time with family and friends, laughing, singing, eating healthy, and moving everyday (Pilates, yoga, swimming, running, workouts, etc). As you can see, wellness consists of much more than just diet, exercise, and rest.

As a psychoneuroimmunologist I have studied how thoughts, emotions, and beliefs affect the body. I was drawn to this field of study because I intuitively knew that there was a direct connection between what I thought and how I felt. Even though no one ever talked about this connection I knew it was there and that I could change the physical by first changing the mental.

The more I studied the more aware I became that the answer to our healthcare crisis lies in a more *holistic approach (which views body-mind-spirit as one)*. This solution enhances health and well-being in a way that is more cost effective while, at the same time supports the body's own ability to heal.

A ***new philosophy of healthcare*** must be created which will allow a shift in consciousness to occur. It is at this higher level of consciousness that we will find the solutions we seek. We will discover that the solutions were *inside* of us all the time.

Part 1

Our Current Beliefs
about Health and Wellness

Chapter I

Healthcare... How We Got Here

Long before the 17th century people lived in small cooperative communities, in harmony with nature. People understood that the *whole was much greater than the sum of its parts. Everyone understood that Universal Laws (Law of Cause and Effect, Law of Vibration, Law of Unity, Law of Oneness)* governed everything and in order to be healthy and whole they must live in accordance with these Laws. Everything and everyone was created to serve and support the whole and as *a result*, people acted in a way that promoted Highest Good of All.

The world was organic and alive as everything was made up of, and connected by, invisible life force energy. This connection was universal in that what affected one person also affected other people, nature, and the universe at large. These small communities felt a great reverence for the interconnection and interdependence of All things.

Science was created to understand the natural balance of things so that people could live in harmony with Nature and one another; there was a partnership between all of life. Everything was constantly in motion (vibration)...and this *vibrational rhythm* was the heart beat of the Universe. This vibration helped to keep things alive, well, and in balance, just like a mother's heart beat to her unborn child.

Health and wellness were viewed through the lens of *oneness*. People practiced a *holistic* approach to health whereby all aspects of the body-mind-spirit were one and could not be separated out. Everything was systemic; both within the body and the universe, and what affected one area also affected the others.

Through this lens of "oneness" they understood that in order for the physical body to remain healthy they must also keep their thoughts and emotions balanced. In other words, the people understood the creative power of their thoughts and emotions and knew they must focus on the *good* in order for *good* things to happen. People truly understood the power of gratitude, giving, compassion, and kindness, to bring about health and happiness in their lives.

As a result, the people of this day and age understood the importance of spending more time "being" and less time "doing." By "being" I mean focusing on the moment, opening their heart, aligning their thoughts and emotions with Highest Good. These people understand the value of "being" grateful, being loving, and being silent (so they can listen).

The cultural expectation was that people worked on themselves in order to become the best they could be. "Being" mindful of what they were thinking, feeling, saying, and doing in each moment was guided by their keen awareness of how their presence on this earth had an affect on everything. Every thought and feeling created something... either adding to their own health, and the health of the earth, or not.

* * *

After the 17th century, the world operated according to Isaac Newton's view of the world. Under this new philosophy the world was seen in a very different light. The mind, body, and spirit were thought to be separate from each other; it was believed that nothing moved unless acted upon; and the only "reality" was things that could be measured and quantified.

The scientific method was born which gave us a systematic way of testing, analyzing, and proving things; however, this came at the expense of the subjective side of life. Our thoughts, emotions, beliefs, and perceptions were removed from the equation on how to live ...in other words, we removed the part of what makes us *who we are*.

We went from a world that was alive, organic, constantly moving, and connected to a world in which everything from the solar system to the human body were conceptualized as a giant machine—made up of different pieces and parts. The parts were all believed to be separate but when put together they equaled the whole (machine).

We went from a prevailing culture of partnership where everyone and everything was constantly working for the good of the whole to a culture where domination over nature, people, and the human body was the preferred practice.

The medical model was focused on fixing the broken machine (body) and not on restoring balance to the whole (body/mind/spirit). It was believed that the physical body had absolutely nothing to do with one's thoughts, emotions, and beliefs. Since then this notion of separation has dominated the Western world in science, medicine, philosophy, and psychology.

The 19th and 20th centuries saw remarkable discoveries in disease diagnosis and treatment, which helped to eliminate many fatal diseases; however, while physicians can point to outstanding successes in combating diseases such as cholera and polio, the impact of *stress* on our health remains an ever growing problem. The main reason for this is that stress is our perception of the situation, and not the situation itself. It is our perception of our ability to handle the situation, or not, that creates stress.

In other words, it is our *thoughts (perceptions) and emotions* that have a direct affect on the physical body. Until everyone, both practitioners and lay people begin to understand this basic concept…stress is going to remain a significant challenge in Western medicine.

In the past 30 years, research has shown the connection between the mind (thoughts, perceptions, and beliefs) and all the systems in the body and has begun to challenge the prevailing philosophy of separation; however, today the separation of mind, body, and spirit remains firmly entrenched in Western medicine.

Chapter 2

Challenges Facing
Our Current Healthcare

The lens through which we choose to see ourselves and the world determines the outcome. When we look at a 3-dimensial body without first putting on our 3-D glasses we see only pieces and parts of the whole…not the whole. We see things in isolation, and thus never really grasp the whole picture!

David Bohm (modern day physicist) views this *separation of mind and body* as the most critical of the many challenges facing the Western world. At the sub-atomic level mind and matter is the same thing…energy! The implication for healthcare is that the mind and body do not operate independently. The body, mind, emotions, and spirit continually interact and therefore, from a health perspective, there can be no real separation of body, mind, emotions, and spirit in how we assess, diagnosis, or treat individuals.

Western medicine has made tremendous strides in understanding the "technical" side of many medical conditions; however, what has not been as clearly understood is this question of how our thoughts, emotions, beliefs, and perceptions enhance and maintain health, or not. Just about every challenge we face in Western medicine is related to this **perceived**

"separation" in some way.

The second challenge facing our current healthcare system is the *rising cost,* which in many cases leads to the inability of people to pay for the service. Despite enormous achievements that have been realized over the last two centuries, working from a mindset of "separation," the process has become extremely expensive. With an increase in the use of expensive medical technology for screening, assessing, diagnosing, and treating individuals, healthcare spending now exceeds 15% of the U.S. gross domestic product (GDP) and economists predict that by 2015, healthcare costs may reach 20% of the GDP.

The third challenge facing our current healthcare is that it has changed from a **healing profession** to a **high dollar business.** The focus is usually on how much does it cost and who will pay for it; instead of how effective is the treatment? It appears, in many cases, that as the cost goes up the effectiveness goes down.

The fourth challenge facing our current healthcare system is that more emphasis is placed on *"outside" fixes* than **"inside"** changes. By outside fixes I am referring to such things as pills, surgery, and modern technology which drives up the cost of healthcare, and often times usurps the body's ability to heal. By inside changes, on the other hand, I am referring to using the power of thoughts, emotions, and beliefs to aid in healing, as well as, reduce stress. These inside techniques teach self care at a very low cost. It appears that the more we rely on outside "fixes", the less responsibility we take for engaging in self care to bring about balance.

More healthcare practitioners are finding themselves at a loss for effective solutions to many of the medical conditions such as depression, obesity, heart disease, cancer, arthritis, and autoimmune diseases. From a larger perspective it appears that these physical conditions are the result of a "spiritual crisis" in which humankind focus *more* on war, violence, and economic power, domination of nature, disease, and materialism than they do love, kindness, compassion, health, and service to others.

This spiritual crisis creates a "void" that is felt deep within which often times leads to a loss of connection to oneself, other people, nature, and a Higher Source. As a result people experience a loss of fulfillment in life, loss of purpose and meaning, and loss of joy and happiness which creates dis-ease in the body and is contrary to supporting the healer within. In our current Western healthcare we are at a loss as to how to re-connect.

The fifth challenge is the lack of truly *preventive solutions.* Our current healthcare system spends approximately 96% of the GDP on treatment and only 4% on prevention. What is wrong with this picture? What is even more challenging is that when we do spend money on prevention, in many cases, it is what I call "deficit" prevention. By this I mean we continue to research and study **disease**, *but if* what we focus on expands...should we not be studying *health*? Why do we spend money on trying to *prevent disease* instead of *promoting health*? Big difference! Remember, *what we focus on expands*! Healthcare needs to be about promoting self-care...**supporting the healer within!**

The sixth challenge in healthcare is that we consistently use *"linear" thinking* to explain, diagnose, and treat something that is anything but *linear*! By "linear" I mean that we expect things to develop in sequence from what we can see on the outside without any in-depth understanding of how everything works from the inside. Health and disease are not linear in any way!

A rather good example of linear thinking is the scientific method. It was good in that it created a systematic way to objectively test and prove how things work, to some degree; however, this was at the expense of the *subjective* side of life...the part of life that *makes us who we are.*

Think about this for a minute. When you think about what makes you who you are...what comes to mind? Do you think about the things you love to do, the people you love, the experiences and memories that make you feel good? Or do you immediately think about your jugular vein, your frontal lobe, or the vertebrae in your spine? Of course not!

The point I am trying to make here is that, for the most part, we are all made up of the same pieces and parts...right? What makes us all different is our thoughts, feeling, beliefs, and experiences. So if you want to understand how the body works you must include thoughts, feelings, beliefs, hopes, dreams, fears, and worries in the equation.

The future of medicine will depend on our ability to put the *subjective* thoughts, emotions, beliefs, and perceptions back into the equation on how to be healthy and whole.

Not only have we removed thoughts, emotions, and beliefs from the equation of life we have devalued the use of intuition. In most societies, outside of the Western world, intuition and wisdom are highly regarded as a means for bringing about health and wholeness. The HeartMath Institute has shown that the heart has the ability to intuitively detect what will happen before it happens. This innate ability is what connects us to the Universal Mind, the Earth, and each other.

The seventh challenge is that, for the most part, people in the west do not understand how the world *actually* works. Many people are sitting around waiting for the world to change— while at the same time complaining that nothing ever gets any better. They think that the problems we face in the world are "too big" for their actions to have any affect.

The current mentality is that in order to have world peace people believe the solution lies in building bigger missiles and armies. Along these same lines, they think that healthcare reform will come from basically three things: first, by hiring enough doctors who are highly specialized in everything imaginable;

second, by developing more advanced technology; and third, by creating more "high powered" drugs. (For those of you who are asking the question, "So am I saying we do not need doctors and new technology?" The answer is NO, I am not saying that at all).

What I am saying is that *life is an inside job...!* World peace will come from inner peace—having peaceful thoughts, emotions, and beliefs. Healthcare reform will come about when we create a new philosophy that is based on the concept that our thoughts and emotions have a tremendous affect on the physical body; and that the body-mind-spirit is not separate—but, in fact, one thing!

Chapter 3

How the World Actually Works

How does it all work? When we shift our view of the world from one of "lack and limitation" to a belief in "abundance and possibilities" we create a magnetic energy force that will bring back to us more of the same. We live in an *attraction based universe*—so **what we focus on expands**. In order for us to recognize our *true power* we must understand how it all works. Allow me to explain.

For thousands of years, Masters like Jesus, Buddha, and Krishna (just to name a few) taught people that the world actually operates according to Universal Laws which are sometimes referred to as Natural or Spiritual Laws. The Law of Cause and Effect; Law of Attraction; Law of Vibration; As Above, So Below; As Within, So Without; Law of Gravity, etc., are all examples of these Universal Laws. These Laws govern everything from the solar systems, gravity, weather, and relationships to the cells in the human body, and everything in between.

Unfortunately, most of us have never been taught how to live in accordance with these Laws. However, there is evidence to show that some ancient cultures did in fact understand and live in accordance with these Laws. Ancient sites have been discovered around the world that were built by mystifying groups of people who displayed skills and wisdom of how the world works that was far advanced for their time. The Mayans and Aztecs are examples of these mystifying groups of people that once lived on the earth.

Where they came from or where they went, no one knows; however, one thing we do know is that they possessed an understanding of how the world works from an energy standpoint which allowed them to live closer to the land, and one another, with an innate understanding of the connection of it *All*.

Ancient texts reveal that everything is in *Perfect Order*; however, it is our *thoughts* that bring chaos to this order! Behind every circumstance, event, or experience is a thought, which creates a feeling that eventually manifests into physical form. It is our *thoughts* and *feelings* that are the blueprint for creation. In fact, the creative force in the universe is our "emotions," as it is our feelings that activate the Law.

With Quantum physics comes a deeper understanding of the wisdom that these mystifying people spoke of thousands of years ago. Everything from our health, relationships, career, finances, hopes and dreams...all are created out of a sphere of *unlimited possibilities*.

Through our imagination, expectations, beliefs, intentions, attentions, passions, hopes, dreams, fears, concerns, or worries we manifest possibility into existence according to their positive or negative nature. Our beliefs about ourselves, each other, and the world... either brings to us our greatest joys or our deepest fears, all in accordance with Universal Laws.

Let me explain how this works. Everything in the universe is made up of energy. At the subatomic level everything is the same and connected to everything else. This energy is always moving, vibrating, and changing; therefore, nothing ever stays the same. As a result, this change can occur in two ways. The first is change by *intention or conscious awareness*; the second is change by *default*. When we focus our intention on what we want to see happen, the change will be aligned with that intention. On the other hand, when our thoughts and feelings are random with no focused intent, the results will resemble the chaos in which they were created.

Universal Laws teach us that everything happens first mentally (within), and second physically (outside); however, we have created a civilization that places more emphasis and focus on the world *around us* and less on the world *within us*. We spend millions of dollars battling disease from the outside, instead of promoting health from within. We spend an enormous amount of money buying bigger missiles in an effort to bring about world peace. Ironically in doing so, we move further away from the balance that we seek.

The thing we must remember is that *life is an inside job*...anyway you slice it. We will find the balance we seek when we focus on changing the *"inside"* and not the *"outside."* When we have grateful, healthy, life affirming thoughts about ourselves we will have healthier bodies; likewise, when we *all* have peaceful thoughts we will have more peace in the world. *What we focus on expands*! So shouldn't the focus be on health and world peace—and not disease and war?

An example of looking *inside* to make changes on the *outside is i*n order to change what other people think and feel about you, you must first change what you think and feel about yourself. With a small shift in your awareness of how it all works you can tap into the most powerful force in the universe to change what might seem like an impossible situation. This happens when we begin to see ourselves as co-creator in this world and not simply an observer.

The energy of our thoughts and feelings is *creative* and *magnetic* in nature. The energy we send out in the form of thoughts and feeling comes back to us magnified. We have all heard the phrase, "what goes around, comes around," this is the scientific explanation. In order to make changes in our lives we must begin to see ourselves as we want to be. When we focus on what we want we get more of that. *Remember, what we focus on expands!*

The subconscious mind drives the body and moves energy from non-physical to physical. The subconscious mind cannot translate "don't," "not," and "no"; therefore, when we focus on what we *don't want*, or we beat ourselves up because of past experiences, we create the energy/circumstances to bring more of what we don't want. The tapes we play, over and over in our mind, are planted in the subconscious mind and these *instructions or desires* are carried out to the minutest detail. In some respects, the subconscious mind is like a glorified "GPS," you program in the coordinates (positive and negative thoughts) and it drives the body to your destination all according to your thoughts and emotions!

It is important to watch your self-talk!! One of the ways the conscious mind influences the subconscious mind is through our self-talk. The internal conversations we have about ourselves, our relationships, our finances, our jobs, and the world—all have a profound affect on what happens in our lives.

Many times we think we are being positive by saying, "I don't want to be sick, or I don't want to fail." However, knowing that the subconscious mind cannot translate "don't" the focus of both statements are "sick" and "fail," respectively. Why not say to yourself, "I want to be healthy" or "I want to succeed." Now look at the focus…it is on "health" and "success" which is a big difference—especially when we know that *what we focus on expands!*

At times this concept is hard to grasp as the universe appears to be a random series of complex events of which we have no control. In an effort to make some sense of this randomness, we divide it up into systems and compartments, and then further divide these into smaller pieces and parts. Dividing and subdividing things up is the only way to deal with something that is otherwise overwhelming. Unfortunately this does not work in a quantum world where the *whole* is **always** *greater than the sum of its parts!*

Everything is connected and in perfect order throughout the entire universe! At the subatomic level everything is the same (energy) and is always moving and changing according to our *intentions* and *beliefs;* however, we still live with the *illusion* that we are separate from everything and each other. In order to tap into the creative force of the universe, we must first see ourselves as *part of* the world rather than *separate from* it. This connection is vitally important to the destiny of the universe.

In 1854, Chief Seattle addressed Congress in an attempt to explain the connection of *All* life. He warned of the White Man's need to dominate and destroy the earth (forest and animals) saying that this destruction would upset the natural balance of the earth and would be felt for generations to come.

Chief Seattle's innate wisdom was far advanced from our current understanding of the role we play in this big universe. Through this wisdom he stated, "Man did not weave the web of life—he is merely a strand in it. Whatever he does to the web, he does to himself."

The BP oil spill in the gulf waters in April of 2010 is a great example of what Chief Seattle warned of. This oil spill created a tremendous imbalance in the earth's energy and this imbalance will have to be corrected in the future. In actuality, this imbalance will be felt not only on earth but throughout the universe— as everything is connected. Since most people do not understand how this energy works they do not see the harm we create in our need to dominate and purge the earth.

In reality *nothing happens by chance, instead* everything happens for a *reason as each event carries with it a lesson to teach us something.* There are many things to be learned from this. We must begin to see the connection of everything and understand the fact that we are not the center of the universe but merely a speck in it. Everything is alive and connected and in order for things to remain healthy we must consciously be aware of the affect we have on the health or destruction of this planet. You see, as a result of everything being connected...the health of the planet has an affect on the **health of our bodies**.

Each experience is there to teach us something to *make us better* than we were before. When we focus on the lesson (the good) we set in motion the energy that will bring us the solution that is aligned with our Highest Good.

Manifesting what we want to see happen begins with the willingness to make room in our beliefs for something that supposedly does not exist. Remember, the concrete events of life must first be envisioned as *"possibilities"* before they can manifest as *reality*. We cannot experience something that is beyond the boundaries of our current belief system; therefore, we must widen our beliefs about what is possible, then align our thoughts and feeling with what we want to see happen...! Lastly, we must believe it is possible!

Part 2

*Creating a New Philosophy: Changing
the Way We View and Deliver Healthcare*

Chapter 4

Principle 1:
Supporting the Healer Within

One of the most important concepts, both practitioners and lay people alike need to truly understand and apply, is the idea that the **body has the ability to heal.** Think about this for a minute. Even when the most skilled surgeon operates on a patient, when the surgery is done, it then becomes a game of "sit and wait." The doctor does not heal the body—but is the facilitator of the healer within!

Therefore, everything that is done should be in an effort to **support the healer within!!** The body has its own natural healing devices which are constantly gravitating towards health and wholeness. Practitioners should continually ask themselves, "Is what I am thinking, doing, saying, and believing supporting the person's own ability to heal, or not?" This same practice applies to all of us! We must all be *aware* of what we are thinking, feeling, believing, and saying about ourselves.

In order to do this, both practitioner and lay people must understand how the body works from a holistic perspective. We must understand the concept of how what we think, how we feel, and our connection to other people and a Higher Source— all have a profound affect on the physical body.

One of the most important discoveries in recent years comes from the scientific field of epigenetics which literally means "control above genetics." For years we have believed that genes *determine life* and that we were born with certain genes that would determine everything from our IQ to our personality to our health. Dr. Bruce Lipton in his book titled, "Biology of Belief," talks about how genes do not *determine life, instead they respond to what we think, feel, and believe about ourselves, other people, and the world*! In fact, our genes are turned on and off according to our thoughts and feelings...amazing!

This gives a whole new meaning to the importance of supporting the body's ability to create health and wholeness at the cellular level. It is paramount that practitioners learn to align what they say to their patient with what they **want to see happen**. For example, by saying you would like to see the infection clear up or the tumor to shrink, etc., the practitioner's words can enhance the healing process. It is better for practitioners not to say anything than to say something that reverses the healing process such as "there is nothing more that can be done." Again, it is of utmost importance that the practitioner say to the patient what they want to see happen. Then the patient's role becomes that of visualizing and believing that they can make it happen.

A great example of this was when I was 10 years old I was in a tobogganing accident in the snow. I was sledding down a hill on the back of a toboggan when all of a sudden everyone, except me, jumped off. As it turned out, I went over a 6-8 foot drop off and landed on my back. At the time, I did not know the extent of my injuries.

I chose not to complain about my back pain because by age ten I was already afraid of doctors and hospitals. You see my younger brother had been in the hospital 14 times before he was 4 years old, so as you can imagine the last thing I wanted to do was see a doctor. Therefore, I decided that I would get better on my own. At age 10 I didn't think in terms of never getting better. I spent lots of time visualizing what I did before I hurt my back (competitive swimming, playing basketball, riding horses, etc...) in antici-pation of doing those things again in the near future.

Ten years later I had an x-ray of my back and it showed that I did in fact break the first four lumbar. The point I want to make here is that no one ever told me that I would have pain all my life, or that I would limp as a result of this injury. No one ever said anything that limited my body's ability to heal perfectly! Practitioner's words are a very powerful thing!

I also have many examples over the years of how doctor's words did in fact aid in shutting down my body's ability to heal. Once I had an infected tooth and my dentist painted a dismal picture by referring to my tooth as a "lost cause." He continued by giving me all the reason why he could not save my tooth **INSTEAD** of telling me **what he wanted to see happen**. I did end up losing the tooth but I learned a very valuable lesson from this experience.

As it turned out, I had the opportunity to go through this same experience with another tooth some years later. This time I was prepared to guide the dentist in the direction that would lead to a more favorable outcome. As the dentist proceeded to tell me all the reasons why he would not be able to save my tooth, I stopped him and simply asked that he tell me *"what he would like to see happen, if there were no impossibilities in this world."* This was hard for him to do at first because he could not imagine a world with out limits! In the end the dentist was able to tell what he would like to see happen and my tooth and gum began to heal. Amazing how that works! Practitioner's words are a powerful thing!

The subconscious mind is a powerful thing that can't tell the difference between **real** and **pretend**! As I said before, the subconscious is like a glorified GPS as it records everything you experience. You see it's the subconscious mind that drives everything in the body according to a **blueprint** created by what you think, feel, believe, hear, say, and do.

This is important information to have especially when the practitioners play such an important role in a patient's perception of whether there is **hope** or not. In my numerous years of experience working with people who had various medical conditions, I have seen many times when a person had been given months or weeks to live. The practitioner had done all they knew to do leaving no choice but to deliver the message of hopelessness. It was the patients' *unwillingness* to throw in the towel which lead them to someone else (in some cases another practitioner) who put "**hope**" back into their equation of how to live their life. The patient got better...despite the "perceived" odds of the practitioner.

Many practitioners in Western medicine feel that unless they tell the patient the worst case scenario that they are not being honest. My response to that is, first, their prognosis is usually based solely on Western medical knowledge and not on universal wisdom that consists of a holistic understanding of how energy works. Second, telling a patient *what you want to see happen* is in no way being dishonest. (Last time I checked no doctor has ever been sued for this).Using words of hope, encouragement, compassion, love, and kindness — all support the healer within. Why not? We all know what a message of doom and gloom will do.

The feeling that there is light at the end of the tunnel (hope) is the kind of energy that redirects or engages the body's ability to mend. In the future, practitioners, as well as their patients (all of us), will have to understand and ensure that everything we think, do, say, and believe is aligned with *supporting the healer within*. We must get *out of the business* of removing symptoms in an effort to **eradicate disease** and instead *get in the business* of **enhancing health** by helping people see that their *thoughts, emotions, beliefs,* *and experience lie beneath the surface of these symptoms.* I will talk more about this in chapter 11.

Chapter 5

Principle 2:
Body-Mind-Spirit is ONE

In order to truly *support the healer within* we must broaden our understanding of how the body works to include the concept that there is **no separation between the body, mind, and spirit**. We must understand that all human beings are *multidimensional* consisting of physical, mental, emotional, and spiritual aspects. One of the biggest challenges facing Western medicine today is the fact that, for the most part, both practitioners and lay people focus strictly on the *physical* when looking for the *cause and the cure* of disease.

As you have probably figured out from the information provided so far, this "physical" perspective is very limited in scope, accuracy, and effectiveness. It is much like looking at a 3-dimensional *thing* without first putting on your 3-D glasses. Without them you only see pieces and parts of the whole, not the whole. When practitioners only look at the physical they are missing two-thirds of what makes us human!

Dr. Candace Pert, a brilliant neuroscientist, in her book "Molecules of Emotion: The Science behind Mind-Body Medicine", talks about the fact that what goes on in the mind (thoughts and feelings) is reflected in the body. She says whatever you are feeling (i.e., happy, sad, angry) are reflected in the cells.

Dr. Pert has shown the world that thoughts and feeling are carried throughout the body by messengers known as neurotransmitters and peptides. This chemical information is transferred from the neuro-transmitters and peptides to the cells through receptors located on the surface of the cell. Therefore, our thoughts and emotions exist throughout the body and not just in the brain.

As a result, what a person thinks, feels, believes, fears, loves, hates, enjoys, and dreams about is known throughout the body. Think about this for a minute...what we think and how we feel about ourselves, our situations in life, and other people, all have a tremendous affect on who we are and how we function. So why would you not think that this has an affect on our health? **When we understand how things work at this level we begin to treat the cause and not just the symptom!**

The "numbers" we get from the many tests we perform represent much more than just "physical indicators." These numbers tell us about the mental, emotional, and spiritual challenges we face on a daily basis. They indicate when we feel too much pressure, when we feel out of control, when we feel down and out, and when we feel rejected, unloved, and lonely.

I am not saying that there is no physical problem, as when your cholesterol is 300 there most definitely is an imbalance, but what I am saying is that when you take Lipitor to lower your cholesterol you are only treating the symptoms and not the underlying struggles that caused the cholesterol imbalance in the first place.

In order for us to change healthcare in the future we must all understand that our *thoughts, fears, beliefs, and feelings* have a profound affect on our physical body. What goes on in the mind is reflected in the body; thus developing the ability to picture ourselves as healthy and whole is a *prerequisites* for wellness on every level. Imagine what healthcare would be like if we introduced this idea into the treatment plans!

Knowing all of this, the future of healthcare must ensure that everything is done through the lens of "oneness" — seeing and treating the body-mind-spirit as *one*. This is the only way we can truly *support the healer within*.

Chapter 6

Principle 3:
Everything is Energy!

In order to support the healer within we must truly grasp the concept that *everything in the universe is made up of a subtle invisible energy* which is creative and magnetic by nature. We must understand that everything can be broken down into energy...everything, including our thoughts, beliefs, and feeling. We must understand that this energy can be molded into what we want in life by aligning our thoughts, emotions, and beliefs with what we desire. There really are no limits to what we can create...there are only our *limited thoughts and beliefs*!

Max Planck, father of quantum theory, talks about the fact that there is no such thing as matter; there is only energy moving at different frequencies which creates the *illusion of matter*. The slower the vibration of energy, the more solid it appears.

Our bodies are made of trillions of atoms and each atom is made up of 99.999% space. That is a lot of space! Actually, this space is not "empty" like you might think, instead it is energy that is made up of, and influenced by, what we think and feel, day in and day out.

What is even more amazing is that this energy

exists in a state of *pure potentiality* waiting to be molded into reality. Each one of our 60,000 thoughts a day molds this energy into something...something that moves us closer to health and wholeness, or away from it.

In fact all of nature waits in a state of *possibilities*. It is our thoughts, intentions, expectations, emotions, attitudes, perceptions, and beliefs (energy) which exists at the sub-atomic level that begins to move things from the non-material world to the material world— hence, **what we focus on expands**. This concept holds true for our relationships, finances, careers, and health. So you can see there really is no such thing as just the "physical body", in fact, there really is no such thing as "separation" of any kind.

Positive thoughts consist of a higher, more positive energy than negative thoughts. This is why being in love and giving to others makes you feel good, as it is a higher form of energy. While positive feelings enhance the health of the cell, the opposite is also true. When you are feeling angry or fearful these negative emotions are a lower (energy) vibration which compromises the health of the cells.

Not only does this energy exist within the body, it exists in energy fields around the body. This energy is as vital to our health and well-being as the blood that flows through the veins and arteries and the oxygen that flows through the lungs. Imbalances in these energy fields will lead to imbalances and pain on the physical level.

You see that these *energy fields* that surround the body are also made up of our thoughts, feeling, perceptions, and memories, both the positive ones and the negative ones. Negative feelings, which are a denser and slower energy, when held over a period of time will eventually create blocks in the energy field. These blocks compromise the health of the body on every level.

Remember, cells are made up mostly of energy and this energy is constantly moving or vibrating. So the higher (more positive) the emotion, the higher the vibration... the healthier the cells will be.

It is paramount for healthcare practitioners to understand this and begin to adapt the way in which they interact with patients by recognizing the power of this *energy* to help create dis-ease or health and wholeness. The same thing holds true for lay people as they also need to understand this concept and begin to monitor their own thoughts and feelings to ensure they [thoughts and feelings] are working for them in creating health and happiness.

Another important factor to be incorporated into this "new" healthcare philosophy is for practitioners, and lay people alike, to understand, value, and apply a *variety of holistic healing modalities* in combination with the *best of Western medicine*. Both should be used when appropriate.

It is critical for all practitioners to experience first hand the benefits of a variety of holistic healing modalities and incorporate them into their life. Only when practitioners experience different types of healing modalities can they then speak with more confidence about the benefits.

Since the vibration of the cell is vital to its health, we must incorporate healthcare practices that help to maintain the vibrational integrity of each cell. There are a number of healing modalities which are based on balancing the energy within, and around, the body.

Acupuncture and Reiki are two examples of very effective energy-based approaches to balancing and maintaining the health (*energy*) of a cell. Remember, high vibrational energy is vital to the health of each cell. Acupuncture uses very small needles inserted at various energy points on the body and along meridians (energy lines), to release and re-balance blocked energy. This so called blocked energy causes pain and illness in the body. When this subtle energy is allowed to flow freely throughout the body the cells, tissues, organs, and systems can function at their best.

Reiki is a technique that is also used to release blocked energy, around and within the body. The Reiki practitioner places his or her hands either on or a few inches above the recipient's body. Healing subtle energy flows from the Reiki practitioner to the recipient in an effort to move and re-balance the energy of the recipient. Reiki promotes healing and health by removing blockages and toxins which then allows all the systems in the body to function properly.

In quantum physics there is a phenomenon called *entrainment*. Entrainment is when two objects are vibrating at different frequencies, when held close together the lower frequency will begin to vibrate at the higher frequency. This same principle holds true in Reiki. The Reiki practitioner sets his or her intention for Highest Good of the recipient which allows this high vibrational energy to be sent to recipient. In turn, this higher energy transforms the lower energy to a higher form which in effect releases the blockages. This then allows the energy to flow freely restoring balance back to the body.

Currently, for the most part, these holistic approaches are not recognized by many Western medical practitioners as being an effective means of treatment because of the lack of knowledge on how energy works. However, in order for our current healthcare system to become highly effective, truly preventive, as well as, cost effective, we are going to have to do more than treat the symptoms. We are going to have to look at how thoughts, emotions, and beliefs affect our health and well-being from an energy standpoint.

Chapter 7

Principle 4:
Focus on Health Enhancement
Not Disease Management

The emphasis in healthcare should always be on *promoting health* and *not managing disease.* This means assessing strengths (what is working for people), understanding their joys, hopes, dreams, as well as, fears, concerns, aches, and pains. Instead of focusing on eliminating symptoms of the disease, we should help people explore how *their thoughts, emotions, beliefs, perceptions have a tremendous affect on their own health and well-being.*

The emphasis, in both *assessment and treatment,* must shifts from *risk factors for disease* (such as high blood pressure or high cholesterol) to what we call factors that promote or enhance *health.* We should focus on things that enhance people's sense of purpose and meaning in life, what people are passionate about, what brings a big smile to their face, what makes people laugh out loud, what pulls on their heart strings, their connection to other people and to nature... just to name a few. Why not study how these things lower stress and help to balance the body, mind, and spirit?

The emphasis on *health enhancement factors* is

reflected in the belief that for most people, purpose and meaning in life, connection to a higher source, and relationships are the primary *determinants of health*.

In stating a case for health promotion vs disease management we must remember one of the "cardinal rules" in physics which is, *what you focus on expands*. Think about this for a minute. Then why in Western medicine do we spend most of our research and treatment dollars focused on *disease* while most other countries research and study *health*?

We develop a list of risk factors that supposedly identify a certain type of disease. The absence or presence of these factors is how we determine whether or not a person has a particular type of disease or condition. We continue to focus on this list of risk factors even when much of the research shows that many of the "agreed upon" risk factors are not good indicators of who does, and does not, get that particular disease.

The weakness in this type of reasoning is that this "determination" is usually done in isolation of the whole. By that I mean these risk factors such as high blood pressure and high cholesterol are seen as purely physical markers viewed in isolation of the mental, emotional, and spiritual aspects of what makes us human. Here again, this is the case where we are looking at a 3-D body without first putting on our 3-D glasses...resulting in our inability to see the whole.

Knowing that our thoughts and emotions are felt throughout the body, we must be open to creating a new way of diagnosing conditions in the body from a holistic perspective. Furthermore, since the body is constantly changing, the numbers that we obtain in testing are always changing as well. Your cholesterol can change 100 points in 10 minutes, so *why all this obsession with testing?*

I know that someone reading this right now might be asking, "Does this mean we should not test people?" I am in no way saying that we should give up testing and measuring bio markers in the body, but what I am saying is that we need to put these *numbers* into perspective. Instead of basing most of our decisions on these numbers, we need to put them in context of the whole. *It is not the numbers that create the problem...it is what we do with the numbers that can either enhance the body's ability to heal... or shut it down.*

Currently we wage war on disease and everything associated with it. We use terminology such as control, blast, kill, and eradicate when referring to disease in the body. This sort of strategy is usually very expensive and in many cases decreases quality of life. The question that comes to mind is, "How does this type of approach support the healer within?" The answer is simple, "It doesn't."

Interesting enough, the more we wage war on disease, the more disease we get. Remember, *what we focus on expands!* Think about this for a minute. When has fighting a war ever created peace? When has fighting stress ever created balance? When has fighting disease ever created health? The answer to all of these questions is "never"!

The reason for this is because when we declare war on something it is almost always done so out of fear. Studying disease is also based out of fear and one thing we know for sure is that fear kills! Why not focus on *factors that create and support health?*

If healthcare is going to improve it is paramount that we let go of our outdated beliefs of "old science" (Newton physics) and replace them with the beliefs of a "new science" based on energy and how thoughts, emotions, and beliefs affect health.

When we understand how this energy works we will be empowered to use our thoughts, emotions, and beliefs as **tools** to make us the best we can be! This is certainly one of the missing links in our current equation of how to live a healthy, fulfilling life. Knowing that our thoughts and emotions make us who we are, and knowing that what we focus on expands, then we must always find ways to focus on health!

Chapter 8

Principle 5: Prevention is Self Care

Healthcare becomes *self care* when people take responsibility for their own health and well-being. In order for people to take responsibility for their own health they have to understand the role of their thoughts and emotions in creating health and disease. With this "understanding" comes **true prevention**.

There must be a paradigm shift in the way we define and work towards prevention if we are going to change the course of healthcare. In our current healthcare system we spend approximately 96% of our healthcare dollars on treatment and 4% on prevention. What is wrong with this picture? Everything!

Currently what we call prevention in Western medicine is really "detection," for the most part. When we administer a series of test and uncover the fact that there is a blocked artery...that is NOT prevention. You could argue that by discovering someone has heart disease might "prevent" them from having a heart attack...but why not work to prevent the heart disease in the first place? Until the traditional practices and beliefs about how the body works expands to include a more holistic view, the only real prevention tools we have are immunizations, diet, exercise, and rest.

From a holistic perspective the *focus of true prevention* must be on *supporting health and wellness,* not *avoiding disease.* Some examples of prevention are understanding how the following positively affects our health: spending time with loved ones and friends; getting out in nature; living life with joy and gratitude; deep breathing; yoga; gentle movement; visualizations; affirmations; playing; laughing; meditating; acupuncture; relaxations techniques; chiropractic treatments; finding purpose and meaning in life; singing; dancing; maintaining a positive outlook on life and health; education and information; appropriate immunizations; enough rest; and eating healthy. All of these support the healer within!

True prevention is not what we do on the outside to avoid or minimize disease; instead it is what we do on the inside to create a sense of well-being and health. We now know, for the most part, that disease is not caused by something outside that invades the body, but it is an imbalance created within the body. Dr. Bruce Lipton in his wonderful book, "Biology of Belief" talks about the fact that bacteria cannot enter a healthy cell because it is vibrating too fast for the slower moving bacteria. A good analogy of this would be if you were driving down the interstate at 70 miles per hour in a van with the side door open, you could not jump in. However, if the van was only moving one mile per hour you could get in the van. This same idea applies to cells and bacteria.

As I have said before, positive thoughts and feeling have a higher vibrational energy which keeps the cells healthy and alive. On the flip side, negative thoughts and feelings have a lower energy which compromises the health of the cell. So much of prevention lies in our ability to see the good in others and the good in our experiences.

True prevention is teaching people to see themselves as they want to be. It is widening their current belief system to be able to "see" they can be or do anything they can conceive of in their mind. As Dr. Wayne Dyer said in an excellent book he titled, "You'll See It When You Believe It." Think about this for a minute...isn't this just the opposite from what you have been taught all your life?

Dr. David Hawkins talks about "attractor fields" in his wonderful book titled, "Power vs Force." The pictures, images, and feelings that we hold in our mind and heart are the very situations, people, experiences, and resources that we attract back to us. Like attracts like! By understanding this concept we can learn to use our thoughts, feelings, and beliefs as tools to help create balance and health.

Welcome to a quantum world...where our thoughts, feelings, and beliefs are the creative forces behind everything we see in our world. So you see, *true prevention* is an inside job!

Chapter 9

Principle 6:
Practitioner-Patient Relationship

In order to change our current healthcare system, practitioners and lay people must see themselves and other people as *"healthy and whole"* and not as a certain type of disease or symptom. They must understand that their own *intentions, thoughts, words, attitudes, and beliefs have a profound affect on the healing process.*

We all give off "energy" (made up of thoughts and feelings at that particular point in time) which is felt throughout our own body first, then by other people, and the world. This energy either enhances our health and well-being, other people, and the world... or not! As a result, it is imperative for our own health, as well as the health of others, that we monitor what we are "sending out."

Understanding this is critical in every relationship, but particularly important in a practitioner/patient relationship. Think about what is important in any relationship: trust, caring, kindness, open communication, empowerment, attention, and listening. A practitioner/patient relationship is no exception.

Next, healthcare practitioner and lay people must know the importance of *meeting people where they are* in order to help them make desired changes in their life. Holistic healthcare must be grounded *in principles like compassion, kindness, respect, and love.* Practitioners must **come from the heart** in everything they think, feel, believe, say, and do. The *practitioners/ patient relationship* must be one of caring and respect in which each party brings some type of expertise and wisdom to the relationship. It is one of collaboration, not compliance.

There is great value in both *knowledge and wisdom* (intuition). In every form of medicine, outside of Western allopathic medicine, intuition is highly valued in the healing process (both within the patient and the practitioner).

Larry Dossey, M.D., in his magnificent book titled, "The Science Behind the Power of Premonitions: How Knowing the Future Can Shape Our Lives" shows how one missing link to changing healthcare is the inability to open our hearts and minds to this wisdom (intuitive "knowing") that lies beneath the surface of how we currently view things in healthcare. We must ALL learn to value and apply this internal wisdom.

Another important point to understand and apply is that supporting the body's ability to heal also means that the environment of the practitioners' office must be conducive to healing—music, aroma, running water, soothing colors, positive attitudes, informative and encouraging written materials, etc. It must be a place where you feel welcome and can relax.

Several years ago I was referred to an oncologist in

a nearby city. I went as a favor to a friend of mine who was also an MD. My doctor friend wanted me to cover all the bases before deciding on my treatment for colon cancer. When I entered the oncologist's office I was immediately aware of a deep sense of "doom and gloom." It appeared that everyone there was consumed with the fear of cancer and/or dying. The energy of the room was very heavy and full of "hopelessness."

It was all I could do to just sit there and wait my turn. Several times I had to walk outside to get a breath of fresh air. I laughed to myself because my behavior was like someone who needed a cigarette! In fact, when it was my turn to be seen, the woman conducting the intake asked me two different times if I smoked! Of course the answer each time was NO, but what I wanted to say was no I was not *smoking*, but *chocking* on the negativity in the waiting room! I'm not sure she would have understood.

The waiting room had only one window and no live plants. The music reminded me of a dentist office (talk about fear!!), and fear and apprehension filled the air. Nothing in the waiting room reminded me of life or health instead everything was geared towards death and fear. I remember thinking, how in world does any of this send a message to my body of health and well-being?

Many of the people were clearly in the "victim stage." (Remember there is no such thing as "blame," there is just information to help you get better!). That is because they had never been taught how the world actually works. They did not know how thoughts, emotions, and beliefs have an affect on the cells in the body. They simply did not know what happens when you hold onto negative emotions.

As if that wasn't enough, the nurse asked me if I wanted to join the "I'm a cancer survivor" club...! OMG! Let's look at this for a minute. If what I focus on expands...then why in the world would I want to be part of a "cancer club"? The focus of that being "cancer"!!! Is this what I want? Please do not misunderstand me, I am all for support groups as long as they focus on the positive...in this case HEALTH and LIFE!

As you can see, this type of thinking has to change in order for us to be healthy and whole. We must learn how the world works according to Universal Laws and then align what we think, feel, believe, say, and do with these Laws! When we do not live in accordance with these Laws we create a huge imbalance in the body. We must focus on **what we want to see happen** which will help to restore balance.

We must create environments, both in our office and at home, to reflect health, wholeness, and life. We must bring in things from nature that make us feel good, like fresh flowers, live plants, running water, natural sun light, and beautiful pictures. We need to have written materials that make us laugh and feel good and teach us how to live healthy, fulfilling lives. Music that makes us feel alive, and above all, people that give off positive, supportive, loving energy. You know, the type of energy we want to be around.

Chapter 10

Principle 7:
Wellness Begins with Education

(The word doctor means to "teach")

One of the most important roles of a healthcare practitioner is to *teach*! We cannot be actively involved in our own health and well-being if we do not understand the "rules." By rules I mean the Laws under which things work. As I have said many times throughout this book, it is critical that we understand the role our thoughts, intentions, emotions, and beliefs play in both health and disease.

Information and knowledge lead to *empowerment!* Empowerment is the belief that we can have control over the outcome. It is imperative that everything we do, both as practitioners and lay people, be aligned with empowering ourselves and others to make choices that will create health and well-being in all areas of our life. This can only happen when we take a completely different look at the role of disease in our life.

Practitioners must teach people to see their illnesses as a *turning point,* and not *the end. We must teach people that illness can be seen as an opportunity to take another path in life.* In addition, illness can challenge our beliefs about purpose and meaning in life; therefore, h*ow this challenge is viewed, and the steps we take to move forward, will determine the course of the illness and our future.*

Practitioners must engage their patients in a discussion of the *underlying meaning* of their condition. Knowing that thoughts and feeling are stored in the cells, we must begin by asking questions like, "Why do you think your back hurts"? "What might this condition be teaching you"? "What might you learn from this"? "What are the types of feelings, experiences, and memories you hold onto"?

While these questions might sound silly, the answers hold valuable insights in to the underlying meaning of our aches and pains. We must all understand that our thoughts and feeling are in fact felt throughout the body as everything in this entire universe is connected; the body/mind/spirit is no exception. This is what we must teach!

Most people know something about nutrition, the benefits of enough sleep, and the importance of exercising/moving the body...but do we know how our thoughts, emotions, and beliefs about ourselves, other people, and the world, affects these processes? This is what we need to be teaching!

Let's take nutrition for example. For the most part we know that fresh and raw foods are very good for the body. But why is that? It is because the "Life Force" that is in all living things is still present in food that comes out of the earth and has not been cooked or processed in some way. Remember, everything is energy so the more natural it is the more Life Force it has.

Did you know that it is just as important *HOW* we eat as *WHAT* we eat? By this I mean, if we are stressed or angry when we eat, the body goes into a fight or flight mode. This causes the digestive system to shut down as the blood is diverted to the large muscles in an effort to run or fight! For the most part, the food then sits in the stomach, turns to sludge, and is absorbed into the intestines as toxins. So we must learn to eat with *gratitude* which supports the digestive system to function optimally.

We must also teach that what we are thinking and feeling also affects our sleep. We all know that sound sleep is important for the growth and repair of the body. When we are stressed, fearful, or angry, these negative thoughts and feelings disrupt our healthy sleep patterns. Instead of the body going into "growth and repair" function it ends up in "wear and tear" mode, as this is what happens when the body experiences the fight or flight response.

As for exercising and moving the body, this is vitally important to our health and well-being. Remember, we are made up of energy that is constantly moving; therefore, in order to be healthy we must move! Everything in Nature must move in order to be healthy as stagnation leads to decay.

We must take every opportunity to teach how the body, mind, and spirit are connected on every level. It is no longer acceptable in the healthcare world to talk about "numbers" (obtained from test) as a way of diagnosing and treating a human being. These numbers, which are constantly changing as your thoughts and emotions change, only give us a snap shot of the present moment. They will not tell us much about a person, who they really are, what makes them happy or sad, what feeds their soul, or what their future holds. Numbers do play a role in health but it is a very small one. Just remember, numbers should always be used to enhance the healing process, and not shut it down.

We must teach people about the health benefits of meditation, deep breathing, and visualizations and incorporate these techniques into our "bag of tools" for helping people become healthy and whole. We must teach that by using these techniques different hormones, neurotransmitters, and peptides are released that keep the body functioning at its best...and are as effective as any pill we could take, without all the side effects!

In the end, it all boils down to the fact that we must teach people that being healthy, happy, and whole requires a deeper understanding of how everything works in this world of ours. Only when we understand how our thoughts, emotions, and beliefs affect our health and well-being will we be able to change healthcare for the better.

Chapter 11

Principle 8: Sustained Change Comes From Within

The reason people change is a very important factor in whether they will sustain the change over time. On the one hand, for the most part traditional approaches use fear, guilt, and shame to motivate people to change; however, this almost always has a negative affect on the body. As I have said throughout this book, negative emotions lower the vibration or health of a cell. Each thought, and corresponding emotion, travels throughout the body via neurotransmitters which allow the entire body to know your most intimate secrets (instantaneously!)

On the other hand, strategies that promote health utilize the desire to enhance a sense of purpose and enjoyment in life as the reason for creating change. The focus here is building on what makes us happy and what fills us with joy, as a way of motivating us to change things that are not working in our life. Do you see how different the affects of each approach would be on the body?

So what is it that needs to change? We must remember that everything is created first mentally and then physically; therefore, one of the first things that need to change is our thoughts and beliefs about how this world works. In order to make desired changes we must begin to see our self and the world through the lens of possibilities and not limitation. *Change* that comes from *within, which is fueled by positive desires to become the best we can be,* lasts much longer and is much more beneficial than change that is based on *outside* demands such as fear. This is an important concept that must be included in the new philosophy for healthcare.

Along with the *desire* to change we must **believe** we can! This is probably the most important factor in creating sustained change. The reason for this is the subconscious drives the body according to what we believe is possible. If our beliefs about our self, our situation, our health, our finances, our relationships, and the world are very limited in scope...then the results we see will also be limited.

The subconscious mind is a very powerful thing. As a matter of fact, the subconscious mind has ALL the power. Day in and day out it records all your thoughts, feelings, and beliefs and then goes about creating things, in your body and your life, according to what you are thinking and feeling. Pretty simple!

Many times we struggle with change because of our limited thoughts and beliefs; therefore, it is imperative that we identify these limited thoughts and then work to broaden what we believe is possible.

One way to do this is to write down on a sheet of paper what you want to see happen in all areas of your life. You must do this from a "Star Wars" mentality.

That is, write down what you want from the mindset that anything is possible...there are no limits on what you can have, be, or do.

Next go back to each statement and read them one by one, this time using your rational mind. When you read the first one, what is your initial thought or feeling? If it is anything but "YEA, I can do this" — congratulations, you have identified a limited belief!

The good news in this is that now you know where to begin the process of broadening your beliefs about a particular area of your life. Go though this same process with the rest of the things you wrote down. Pretty soon you will have identified where your subconscious mind has placed limits on what you can have, do, and be in this life.

It is important that we be able to "see" ourselves as we want to be, already having made the change. If losing 50 lbs is one of your goals, then any time you think about losing weight you must be able to see yourself 50 pounds lighter. You must be able to see what you look like, what kind of clothes you will be wearing, what you will be doing. Feel what it is like to drive the car, wear different clothes, exercise or play outside, go out to the park or beach...when you are 50 lbs lighter. Remember all of your thoughts are programming the subconscious mind (your GPS) to take you somewhere...all according to what you are thinking.

If you want to make changes, first begin by identifying limited beliefs and then begin to see yourself the way you want to be. Act and feel the part! Be excited that you CAN do this. Remember, **what we focus on expands** in all areas of your life! Everything is created out of what you believe is POSSIBLE!

Practitioners and lay people must learn to apply this principle, both in the way they treat other people, as well as in their own personal lives if they want to help bring about sustained change that will lead to health and well-being.

Chapter 12

Principle 9:
We All Have a Purpose and It Is
Intricately Tied To Our Health

In order to change healthcare, practitioners and lay people must acknowledge and honor the fact that we are all here to serve a specific purpose and that our purpose is intricately tied to our health. Enhancing our sense of purpose and enjoyment in life creates positive "biochemical" changes in the body which promotes balance and health.

Thoughts, in combination with feelings, are a creative energy that manifests our "mental images" (visions) into physical form; therefore, it is of utmost importance that we hold in our mind visions of what "can be." According to Webster Dictionary, *vision* is "the ability to perceive something not actually visible, as through mental acuteness and keen foresight." Vision motivates and guides people to make changes that will lead to the highest good, not only for themselves, but for the greater whole.

It is through our visions/dreams that we can see our greatest potential—what success will look like for ourselves, our families, and communities. Having a vision gives meaning and purpose to life. We all have a specific purpose to fulfill in this life and no one is ever given a vision without the skills and abilities to reach it. The path to discovering our dreams is already within us; it is what brings us great joy. This is the "spiritual" part of who we are and when our daily thoughts, feelings, and actions do **not** align with our "purpose," a void is created deep within. This void or spiritual disconnect can create an imbalance on every level of our being.

When we focus on a vision that **is** aligned with our purpose we begin to gravitate to the activities, people, and ideas that support our purpose. Our vision becomes a "guide" to keep us on track and allows us to move outside our comfort zone to open up to new possibilities and solutions not thought of before.

The most powerful computer or machine in the world cannot come close to the power of the mind (thoughts) and its ability to visualize and create what it focuses on. Many great athletes understand and utilize this power. For example, swimmers see themselves winning the race before they ever leave the starting block and golfers visualize the ball going into the hole before they even swing the club.

Unfortunately many people grew up with feelings of "lack, insecurity, fear, and anxiety" as to what the future holds. Many people spend an enormous amount of time focusing on *what they do not want, hoping to avoid it in some way.* We know that doesn't work!

For the most part, we have been taught to believe that there is a limited supply of everything, that if it is "good" it can only last for so long, and that life will always be a struggle. Many times people construct their visions based out of **fear** of what they do not want instead of out of **passion** for what they do want.

We live in an attraction-based universe which means we can only pull things to us. In other words, we cannot push things away in an effort to avoid them. *What we focus on expands*, even if it is not what we want! Whether we are talking about financial success, relationships, or health...the same principles apply. Where attention goes, energy flows!

Therefore, focus on your dreams and visions of what you want to see happen. The things that we are passionate about and the things we dream about are directly linked to the purpose we have come to fulfill in this lifetime. It is by following and fulfilling our purpose that we find meaning in life. When we discover a deeper meaning in life, beyond ourselves, we gain a sense of well-being and fulfillment that creates health on every level. This is what our "new" healthcare must be about!

Chapter 13

Principle 10:
We Must Use Our Heart to
Create Health and Happiness

For thousands of years people have associated the feeling of love with the heart. Intuitively we all know that "falling in love" or "giving" to someone else makes us feel good. But did you know that when you use your heart to send or receive love you actually enhance the health of your body? Well, it's true!

Love is the strongest power in the universe and in order to create harmony within the body, and the world, we must create it with love from the heart. This means we must align our thoughts, feelings, and actions with love. An open heart filled with love, compassion, and gratitude creates healthy biochemicals which in turn keep the body balanced, healthy, and whole.

The beat of the heart generates a rhythmic electromagnetic energy wave that is felt throughout the entire body, as well as, extending far beyond the body. It is this energy that helps to keep the body balanced and healthy. Remember that everything in the body is energy and vibrates at a certain frequency; therefore, every cell, every tissue, every organ, and all systems of the body are influenced by, and quickly synchronize with, the rhythmic vibration of the heart beat.

Whatever you are thinking and feeling influences the type (vibration) of electromagnetic energy wave that is sent from the heart throughout the body, and beyond. When we open our heart to the feelings of love, gratitude, kindness, and compassion these feeling create a *positive* wave of energy. Likewise, when our thoughts and feelings are negative they create a negative wave of energy. Either way, our feelings synchronize the cells to either a positive (high) vibration of health and wholeness or a lower vibration of dis-ease.

A positive vibration, created by thoughts and feelings of love, compassion, and gratitude, helps to keep blood pressure, heart rate, hormone levels, blood sugar levels, cholesterol, and all other parts of the body functioning at their best. As our moods, attitudes, thoughts, and emotions change, minute by minute, so does the vibration of the energy wave that goes out from the heart. When we are filled with love, compassion, and gratitude the rhythm of the heart beat radiates throughout the body like a beautiful chorus calming, rejuvenating, re-balancing, and healing the entire body.

Dr. David Hawkins, in his book, "Power vs Force" talks about the fact that true *Power* in this world comes from an awareness of how the world actually works. It is an awareness that our thoughts, feelings, intentions, and beliefs create what we see in this world. True power, then, is using our thoughts to create things without effort. Force, on the other hand, creates things by manipulating things on the "outside" which takes a great deal of effort. A good example of force is war.

Hawkins contends that power trumps force... always. If we want to create everything from happiness and health to world peace ...we must do it out of love from our hearts (which is power) and not out of war, fear, and violence (which is force).

When I think of "power" I think of "being"...being grateful, loving, kind, or being compassionate. When we are in a state of "being" we *allow things to happen*. When I think of "force" the first thing that comes to mind is "doing"...doing a job, doing a task, doing a chore. When we are constantly "doing" things we are always *trying to make things happen*. Do you see the difference? This is why we say that by "being" in the flow, we naturally gravitate towards health and wholeness!

We used to think that the brain was the only organ responsible for receiving and processing information; however, thanks to the research done by the HeartMath Institute, we now know that the heart continuously sends signals to the brain to influence its function. Each heart beat goes out as a wave of energy or information that influences the function of the entire body. This "information" helps to keep all systems in balance. In effect the heart actually "thinks"! You know the old saying, as a man thinks in his heart that is what he will become.

So you see the heart is so much more than just a glorified pump. It is our spiritual connection to the earth, other people, and a Higher Source. When we open our hearts and minds for the purpose of serving others, the energy that goes out from the heart not only has a healing effect on the entire body, it has a healing effect in the world.

Chapter 14

Epilogue

Albert Einstein once said, "The problems we face in the world today cannot be solved at the same level of thinking that created them." Truer words have never been spoken. We must raise our level of consciousness (awareness of how things work) in order to create a new philosophy for healthcare. This new philosophy must fit into a quantum world where everything is seen through the lens of "oneness" and where the whole is **much greater than the sum** of its parts, because in actuality, there really are no pieces and parts...there is just energy!

The future of healthcare will depend on our ability to let go of the need to "physically" prove everything. We have literally created a situation where we are unable to "see the forest for the trees"! By this I mean we are so focused on just "the physical" that we can't see how the physical/mental/ emotional/spiritual are all one complete thing and therefore, must be treated that way!

The future of healthcare is dependent on our ability to expand our outdated "scientific method" to include things that cannot be touched, tasted, seen, or proven with our existing technology. If I asked you to tell me *who you really are*...what would you say? Would you say that you were made up of veins, bones, cartilage, and skin or would you describe yourself in terms of what you feel, what makes you happy and sad, what you dream about, the memories you hold onto, and what you are passionate about?

Of course the latter are the things that have the greatest impact on our health and well-being so why do we continue to leave these out of the formula on how to be healthy and whole? It is time to develop a "new" method that puts back the "subjective" part of what makes us human.

The future of our healthcare lies in our ability to understand and apply two of the basic principles upon which this universe operates. First, we must understand that *everything happens for a reason*. In most cases we are unable to see the "cause" of what happens, instead we can only see the "effect"; therefore, this gives the illusion that the event was in fact an "accident" or "coincidence." This is simply not true! Only by looking at how our thoughts, emotions, and beliefs affect the body, will we begin to see the "cause" instead of just the "effect"!

Second, we must understand that *everything happens first mentally, and then physically*. Until we change the philosophy by which we view and treat the human body, we will continue to struggle with disease. We must let go of old paradigms and replace them with a clear understanding that thoughts, emotions, and beliefs are just as important (actually more so) to the onset of disease as *bacteria*. Remember, ***what we focus*** *on expands* both within the body, and the world!

So you see, the responsibility for creating a bright future in healthcare resides with each one of us. We must all open our hearts and minds to possibilities not thought of before. Healthcare reform will not happen as a result of larger budgets, "Star Wars" technology, a miracle pill, more insurance coverage, or smaller co-pays. Instead, healthcare reform will occur when we are able to shift from the need to prove how things work from an **"outside"** perspective to developing a *"knowing"* from within that reminds us of what we have known all along. We are spiritual beings experiencing the world from a human perspective. Only by "going within," tapping into the internal wisdom of our heart will we re-discover our true spiritual power and the fact that the answers to all of our questions have been within us all along. This will be the new philosophy of healthcare!

Steps to Wellness

1. Know that every situation in life is a *Lesson* to teach you something.

2. Develop an understanding of Universal Laws and how they affect your health, well-being, and life.

3. Know that everything can be broken down into *energy* and that everything *moves*!

4. Know that this *energy* is in every cell in the form of mind, emotion, and spirit! Learn how to use this to your advantage.

5. Know that wellness is not solely a question of genetics, diet, exercise, and rest...it is the awareness of the *Power of Thought* to create and control circumstances in your life.

6. Learn to use the art of *Visualizations* to help bring about health, wellness, and balance. Spend time visualizing what you want in life... not what you do not want.

7. Learn to utilize your *Breathing* to help relax the mind and body. This helps to reinforce and support our connection to it All.

8. *Get out in Nature...*! Spending time in Nature enhances your optimal health, well-being, and your connection to it All!

9. Look for *Humor* in everything you do. Learn to laugh at yourself and your experiences—then maximize the health benefits of doing this.

10. Learn to *Be in the Moment...*always! For it is only in the *present* that we find the *gifts* in life.

11. Stress is not what HAPPENS to you; it's what you THINK, and how you FEEL, about what HAPPENS TO YOU.

12. It is important that you be able to "see" yourself as you want to be...having already made the desired change.

13. Develop an understanding of how thoughts affect digestion and nutrition.

14. Understand and be comfortable with the fact that things happen for a reason!

15. Learn to see the good in every person and every situation.

16. Have faith in the fact that *All is Well...*! Know there is Divine Order in this Universe

Further Readings

1. Timeless Healing: The Power and Biology of Belief-by Dr. Herbert Benson.

2. Minding the Body, Mending the Mind—by Joan Borysenko.

3. The Power of the Mind to Heal—by Joan Borysenko.

4. Ageless Body, Timeless Mind—by Deepak Chopra.

5. The Seven Spiritual Laws of Success: A Practical Guide to the Fulfillment of Your Dreams—by Deepak Chopra, MD.

6. The Unconscious Universe-by Deepak Chopra.

7. Anatomy of an Illness—by Norman Cousins.

8. Beyond Illness—by Larry Dossey, MD.

9. Healing Words: The Power of Prayer and the Practice of Medicine— by Larry Dossey, MD.

10. Meaning and Medicine—by Larry Dossey, MD.

11. Recovering the Soul—by Larry Dossey, MD.

12. Space, Time and Medicine—by Larry Dossey, MD.

13. Manifest Your Destiny—by Dr. Wayne Dyer.

14. Pulling Your Own Strings—by Dr. Wayne Dyer.

15. Real Magic—by Dr. Wayne Dyer.

16. Staying on the Path—by Dr. Wayne Dyer.

17. The Sky's the Limit—by Dr. Wayne Dyer.

18. There is a Spiritual Solution to Every Problem—by Dr. Wayne Dyer.

19. Wisdom of the Ages—by Dr. Wayne Dyer.

20. You Will See It When You Believe It—by Dr. Wayne Dyer.

21. Your Erroneous Zones—by Dr. Wayne Dyer.

22. Change Your Thoughts: Change Your Life—by Dr. Wayne Dyer

23. Your Sacred Self—by Dr. Wayne Dyer.

24. Chop Wood, Carry Water: A Guide to Finding Spiritual Fulfillment in Everyday Life—by Rick Fields, Peggy Taylor, Rex Weyler and Rick Ingrasci.

25. Vibrational Medicine for the 21st Century—by Richard Gerber, MD.

26. Vibrational Medicine: New Choices for Healing Ourselves—by Richard Gerber, MD.

27. Power vs Force—by David Hawkins, MD.

28. Heal Your Body—by Louise Hay.

29. Infinite Mind: Science of Human Vibrations of Consciousness—by Valerie Hunt.

30. Biology of Belief—Bruce Lipton, Ph.D.

31. Meditation as Medicine: Activate the Power of Your Natural Healing Force—by Dharma Singh Khalsa, MD.

32. Spiritual Aspects of the Healing Arts—by Dora Kunz.

33. Mutant Message Down Under—by Marlo Margan.

34. Molecules of Emotion: The Science Behind Mind-Body Medicine—by Candace Pert.

35. Your Body Speaks Your Mind: How Your Thoughts and Emotions Affect Your Health— by Debbie Shapiro.

36. Love, Medicine and Miracles: Lessons Learned About Self-Healing from a Surgeon's Experience with Exceptional Patients—by Bernie Siegal.

37. The Healing Journey—by Carl Simonton.

38. Spontaneous Healing: How to Discover and Enhance Your Body's Natural Ability to Maintain and Heal Itself—by Andrew Weil.

39. Where You Go, There You Are—by Jon Kabat-Zinn.

40. The Dancing Wu Li Masters: An Overview of the New Physics—by Gary Zukov.

41. Quantum Healing: Exploring the Frontiers of Mind-Body Medicine.

Notes

Balon, R. (2006). Mood, anxiety, and physical illness: Body and mind, or mind and body? *Depression and Anxiety, 23*, 377–387.

Bohm, D. (1990). A new theory of the relationship of mind and matter. *Philosophical Psychology, 3*, 271–286.

Chan, C. L. W., Ng, N. M., How, R. T. H., & Chow, A. Y. M. (2006). East meets West: Applying Eastern spirituality in clinical practice. *Journal of Clinical Nursing, 15*, 822–832.

Connelly, K., MacIsaac, A., & Jelinek, M. V. (2006). The "Tako–tsubo" phenomenon and myocardial infarction. *Southern Medical Journal, 99*(1), 2–3.

Dew, M. A., & DiMartini, A. F. (2005). Psychological disorders and distress after adult cardiothoracic transplantation. *Journal of Cardiovascular Nursing, 20*(55), 551–566.

Dewey, M., Teige, F., Schanpuaff, D., Laule, M., Borges, A. C., & Wernecke, K. D., et al. (2006). Noninvasive detection of coronary artery stenoses with multisclice computed tomography or magnetic resonance imaging. *Annals of Internal Medicine, 145*, 407–415.

Dossey, L. (1992). *Meaning and medicine: Lessons from a doctor's tales of breakthrough and healing.* New York: Bantam Books.

Dossey, L. (2009). *The power of premonitions: Knowing the future can shape our lives.* New York, NY: Penguin Group.

Dyer, W.W. (2001). *You'll see it when you believe it.* New York, NY: HarperCollins.

Gerber, R. (2001). *Vibrational medicine.* Rochester, VT: Bear & Company.

Gilbert, M. D. (2003). Weaving medicine back together: Mind—body medicine in the twenty—first century. *Journal of Alternative and Complementary Medicine, 9,* 563—570.

Guyatt, G. H., & Devereaux, P. J. (2004). A review of heart failure treatment. *Mount Sinai Journal of Medicine, 21*(1), 47—56.

Haldane, E. S. (1955). *The philosophical works of Descartes* (Vol. 1). New York: Dover.

Hawkins, D. R. (2002). *Power vs force: The hidden determinants of human behavior.* Carlsbad, CA: Hay House, Inc.

Jacobs, G. D. (2001). The physiology of mind—body interactions: The stress response and the relaxation response. *Journal of Alternative and Complementary Medicine, 7*(S—1), S83—S92.

Kamarck, T. W., Schwartz, J. E., Shiffman, S., Muldoon, M. F., Sutton—Tyrrell, K., & Janicki, D. L. (2005). Psychosocial stress and cardiovascular risk: What is the role of daily experience? *Journal of Personality, 73*(6), 1—24.

Knox, J., & Gaster, B. (2007). Cietary supplements for the prevention and treatment of coronary artery disease. *Journal of Alternative and Complementary Medicine, 13*(1), 83—95.

Krucoff, M. W., Crater, S. W., Gallup, D., Blankenship, J. C., Cuffe, M., & Guarneri, M., et al. (2005). Music, imagery, touch, and prayer as adjuncts to interventional cardiac care: The Monitoring and actualisation of Noetic trainings (MANTRA) II randomized study. *Lancet, 366,* 211—217.

Lazarus, R.S. (1966). *Psychological stress and the coping process.* New York: McGraw-Hill.

Lipton, B. (2005). The biology of belief: Unleashing the power of consciousness, matter and miracles. Santa Rosa, CA: Elite Books

Maier, S. F., Watkins, L. R., & Fleshner, M. (1994). Psychoimmunology: The interface between behavior, brain, and immunity. *American Psychologist, 49*, 1004—1017.

Marshall, D. A., Walizer, E., & Vernalis, M. N. (2004). Optimal healing environments for chronic cardiovascular disease. *Journal of Alternative and Complementary Medicine, 1*(Suppl. 1), S147—S155.

Pert, C. B. (1997). Molecules of emotion: The science behind mind-body medicine. New York: Simon and Schuster.

Redberg, R. F. (2007). Evidence, appropriateness, and technology assessment in cardiology: A case study of computed tomography. *Health Affairs, 26*(1), 86—95.

Salkeld, E. J. (2005). Holistic physicians' clinical discourse on risk: An ethnographic study. *Medical Anthropology, 24*, 325—347.

Shang, C. (2001). Emerging paradigms in mind—body medicine. *Journal of Alternative and Complementary Medicine, 7*(1), 83—91.

Speredelozzi, N., Baroletti, S., & Fanikos, J. (2007). A review of antithrombotic therapies I acute coronary syndrome. *Formulary Journal, 12*, 150—155.

Taylor, G. J. (2002). Mind—body—environment: George Engel's psychoanalytic approach to psychosomatic medicine. *Australian and New Zealand Journal of Psychiatry*, 36, 449—457.

www.heartmath.org

About the Author

Nancy J. Gordon, Ph.D.
Psychoneuroimmunologist
National Wellness Consultant, Author, Coach, and
   Lecturer

Throughout the course of her career Dr. Gordon has amassed extensive experience in the field of health and wellness. With over 22 years of experience in the field, her role as a consultant is primarily to help people become the best they can be by understanding Universal Laws and the power of their thoughts and emotions to create health, abundance, and success. Dr. Gordon conducts wellness seminars and workshops nationally and internationally and serves as a wellness consultant to businesses, health-organizations, and professional athletes.

BOOKS

O is a symbol of the world, of oneness and unity. In different cultures it also means the "eye," symbolizing knowledge and insight. We aim to publish books that are accessible, constructive and that challenge accepted opinion, both that of academia and the "moral majority."

Our books are available in all good English language bookstores worldwide. If you don't see the book on the shelves ask the bookstore to order it for you, quoting the ISBN number and title. Alternatively you can order online (all major online retail sites carry our titles) or contact the distributor in the relevant country, listed on the copyright page.

See our website **www.o-books.net** for a full list of over 500 titles, growing by 100 a year.

And tune in to myspiritradio.com for our book review radio show, hosted by June-Elleni Laine, where you can listen to the authors discussing their books.

Printed and bound by PG in the USA

USA2019PGIL